BEARS

Sun Bears

Stuart A. Kallen
ABDO & Daughters

visit us at
www.abdopub.com

Published by Abdo & Daughters, 4940 Viking Drive, Suite 622, Edina, Minnesota 55435.

Copyright © 1998 by Abdo Consulting Group, Inc., Pentagon Tower, P.O. Box 36036, Minneapolis, Minnesota 55435 USA. International copyrights reserved in all countries. No part of this book may be reproduced in any form without written permission from the publisher.

Printed in the United States.

Cover and interior Photo credits: Animals, Animals
Natural Selections

Edited by Lori Kinstad Pupeza

Library of Congress Cataloging-in-Publication Data

Kallen, Stuart A., 1955-
  Sun bears / Stuart A. Kallen.
  p. cm -- (Bears)
  Includes index.
  Summary: Describes the physical characteristics, behavior, habitat, and life cycle of this tropical bear, the smallest bear in the world.
  ISBN 1-56239-594-7
  1. Sun bear--Juvenile literature. [1. Sun bear. 2. Bears.] I. Title. II. Series: Kallen, Stuart A.., 1955- Bears.
  QL737.C27K348   1998
  599.74'446--dc20
                96-710
                     CIP
                     AC

Contents

Sun Bears and Their Family

Sun bears are **mammals**. Like humans, they breathe air with lungs, are **warm blooded**, and **nurse** their young with milk.

Bears first **evolved** around 40 million years ago. They were small, meat-eating, tree-climbing animals. The early bears were related to coyotes, wolves, foxes, raccoons, and even dogs. Today, there are eight different **species** of bear. They live in 50 countries on 3 **continents**.

Many people think that bears only come from the northern parts of the world. But there are a few bears that live in the warm areas near the **equator**. Little is known about these bears. The sun bear is one of these mysterious bears of the jungle.

Opposite page: Malayan sun bear.

Size, Shape, and Color

Sun bears are the smallest bears in the world. In the wild, sun bears weigh about 100 pounds (45 kg). Some may weigh up to 143 pounds (65 kg) if kept in a zoo. This tiny bear is no bigger than a black bear **cub**, about 4.5 feet (137 cm) long.

The sun bear is covered with a short, thick, black fur. The coat seems too warm for an animal living in the **tropics**. But the fur sheds rain and mud with great ease. The bear needs this kind of fur because it lives in a tropical rain forest.

The sun bear has short bowlegs. It can stand up on its hind legs. The animal's **muzzle** is sleek and compact. It is grayish-white to orange in color. The feet are tipped with long, curved claws.

Opposite page: The snout of a sun bear.

Where They Live

Sun bears are an **endangered species** that live in Asia and Micronesia. Sun bears live in the forests of the Malay Peninsula, Java, Sumatra, Burma, Borneo, and Thailand. Massive logging of the rain forests have destroyed the sun bear's **habitat**.

Several countries have set aside national parks for sun bears. Hunting sun bears is illegal in most countries, but they are still hunted. There are only about 1,000 sun bears left in the world.

Opposite page: Sun bears are found in the forests of Asia, but there are very few left. Most can only be seen in national parks.

Where Sun Bears Are Found

All sun bears are found on the Malay Peninsula. This area consists of Malaysia, Sumatra, Borneo, and Java. They are also found north of the peninsula in Thailand.

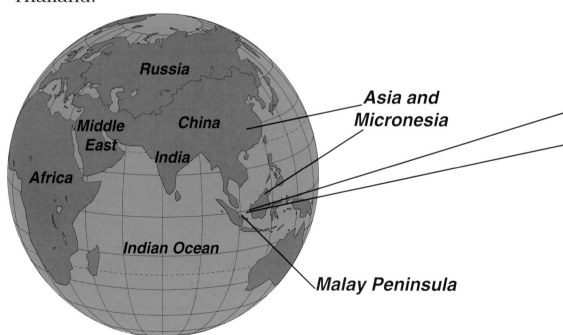

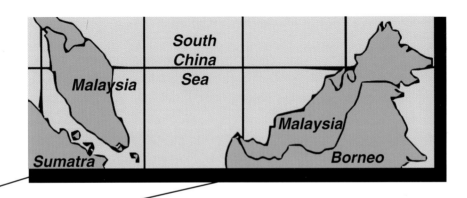

Detail Area

Senses

Sun bears are very smart animals that learn quickly. They are curious and have very good memories.

Because of their small eyes, there is a myth that bears cannot see well. But bears have good eyesight. They can tell the difference between colors and see well at night. They can spot moving objects at a far distance. Bears stand on their hind legs to be able to see farther.

Bears use their sight and hearing, but their sense of smell is their most important sense. Their keen sense of smell allows them to find mates, avoid humans, locate their **cubs**, and gather food. Bears have been known to detect a human scent 14 hours after a person has passed along a trail. Experiments have proven that bears can smell food three miles away!

The sense of smell is important to the sun bear.

Defense

The sun bear is said to be a dangerous animal in the wild. No animal of an equal size is as powerful as a sun bear. It will charge at people for no reason and bite with its powerful jaws. It sometimes tears at an enemy with its sharp claws. Even a jungle tiger will leave a sun bear alone. Sun bears bark loudly when on an attack.

Sun bears spend much of the day sleeping in trees over 20 feet (6 m) above the jungle floor. They build nests in the trees out of sticks and leaves. They go out at night to hunt. Sun bears do not **hibernate**.

Opposite page: The jaw and claws of a sun bear are very strong.

Food

Sun bears will eat just about anything. They eat small rodents, lizards, small birds, or insects. Bees, worms, and termites make up a large part of the sun bear's diet. The bears also eat the heart of coconut palms, which is the large bud at the top of the tree. This kills the tree. Owners of coconut farms will kill a sun bear that eats the tree buds.

Sun bears are fond of honey and will rip open trees to find bees' nests. The bears eat the combs, grubs, and even the bees themselves. In Malaysia, sun bears are called "honey bears."

Opposite page: A sun bear looking for something to eat.

Babies

Female sun bears breed when they are three years old. During breeding season, sun bears will bark, hug, mock fight, and even kiss. Females are pregnant for about 100 days. They give birth to twin **cubs** in a well-hidden nest on the forest floor.

The new cubs are only 7 ounces (225 grams) at birth. They are blind and hairless. At birth, their skin is almost clear. During the first few weeks, the cubs learn to walk. In a few months, they run and play. The cubs stay with their mother until they are almost full grown. Sometimes the father of the cubs will stay with the mother to help raise them.

Opposite page: A female sun bear with her cub.

Sun Bear Facts

Scientific Name: *Helarctos malayanus*

Average Size: About 100 pounds (45 kg). Some may weigh up to 143 pounds (65 kg) if kept in a zoo.

This tiny bear is about 4.5 feet (137 cm) long.

Where They're Found: In the forests of the Malay Peninsula, Java, Sumatra, Burma, Borneo, and Thailand.

Opposite page: Sun bears spend a lot of time in trees.

Glossary

continent (KAHN-tih-nent) – one of the seven main land masses: Europe, Asia, Africa, North America, South America, Australia, and Antarctica.

cub – a baby bear.

endangered species – any type of plant or animal that is threatened with extinction.

equator – the great circle around the middle of the Earth that is half way between the North Pole and the South Pole.

evolve – for a species to develop or change over millions of years.

habitat – the natural environment of a plant or animal.

hibernate – to spend the winter in a deep sleep.

mammal – a class of animals, including humans, that have hair and feed their young milk.

muzzle – the nose, mouth, and jaws of an animal.

nurse – to feed a young animal or child milk from the mother's breast.

prey – an animal hunted and captured for food.

province – a division of a country like a state. Canada is divided into 12 provinces.

species (SPEE-sees) – a group of related living things that have the same basic characteristics.

tropics – the hot and humid areas near the equator.

warm blooded – an animal whose body temperature remains the same and warmer than the outside air or temperature.

Index